# RECEIVING DIRECTION FROM ABOVE

## "DISCERNING THE VOICE OF GOD"

# Glenn Arekion

GLENN AREKION MINISTRIES
PUBLICATION

**Receiving Direction From Above**

© Copyright 2012 by Glenn Arekion

ISBN978-1-943282-08-1


Published by

Glenn Arekion Ministies Publication

PO Box 197777, Louisville, KY 40259 USA

www.glennarekion.org

email: glenn@glennarekion.org

# CONTENTS

RECEIVING DIRECTION FROM ABOVE

4

# DEDICATION

**I dedicate this book to:**

To my Lord and Savior Jesus Christ. You are my God, my King and my Lord

To my fantastic wife, Rosanna, the greatest gift that God ever gave to me

To my three amazing children, thank you for making my life easy.

Lisa, you are my firstborn and my pride

Ethan, you are the greatest son in the world

Jodie, you bring joy to my life.

To my parents, Clency and Marlene Arekion. You are my heroes

To my two brothers, Bruno and James Arekion. I have no words to express how much you mean to me.

To Samuel Reddy, a wonderful executive director and friend. You keep pushing me. I appreciate that. Don't ever stop.

To Pastor Steve & Ida Ebbs. You are always there. Your commitment to me is second to none. Thank you.

To Pastor Kent & Pru Radcliffe. You folks are ever faithful and a blessing

# CHAPTER 1

# GOD WANTS TO SPEAK TO YOU

Job 33:14-19; "For God speaketh once, yea twice, yet man perceiveth it not. In a dream, in a vision of the night, when deep sleep falleth upon men, in slumberings upon the bed; Then he openeth the ears of men, and sealeth their instruction, That he may withdraw man from his purpose, and hide pride from man. He keepeth back his soul from the pit, and his life from perishing by the sword."

Job 33:14; "For God does speak—now one way, now another—though man may not perceive it." New International Version

"For God speaks again and again, though people do not recognize it." New Living Translation

"For God speaks in one way, and in two, though man does not perceive it." English Standard Version

"Indeed God speaks once, or twice, yet no one notices it." New American Standard Bible

God wants to speak to you! He is not a silent God but a speaking God. Some people have the idea that God does not speak today and if he ever was to speak, he would only speak to pastors and people in leadership. Nothing is further from the truth. **GOD WANTS TO SPEAK TO YOU! HE WANTS TO SPEAK TO EVERYBODY.** There are major denominations that repudiate the idea that God speaks today by saying, 'We don't need to hear God's voice. We have the Word, the Holy Bible.' Of course it is true that we have the Bible, but in that same Bible, Jesus said, 'My sheep hear my voice'(John 10:27). The problem that we have today, is not that God does not speak, it is that we cannot hear him or discern his voice. His desire to speak to us is more ardent than our desire to hear from him. Our problem is a hearing, noticing, perceiving or discerning problem

> **Luke 8:8; "...he cried, He that hath ears to hear, let him hear."**

> **Revelation 2:7; "He who has an ear, let him hear what the Spirit says to the churches."**

We all have physical ears at the sides of our head but it is our spiritual ears that need to be opened. In the above Scripture, Job said, God speaks but we do not perceive...". He has been speaking to you all along and it has been your lack of perception that has gotten you in trouble and is keeping you in trouble.

## *Why does God speak to us?*

God is not difficult. He speaks to us in order for us to take the right direction and avoid pitfalls. Most importantly, when God speaks to us it is for our good, as we can see in the verses in the book of Job, 'to keep...life from perishing by the sword'. It can be very costly and even deadly not discerning the voice from above. From the mouth of Job, here are seven things we can extract,

- God speaks more than once to us
- God speaks to us in many ways such as dreams and visions when we cannot perceive his voice
- God speaks to give instructions
- God speaks to withdraw us from our own purposes
- God speaks to keep us from pride which brings a fall
- God speaks to keep us from falling into satan's pits
- God speaks to preserve our lives

In order to discern the voice of God, one thing is for certain, you must become more acquainted with the Holy Spirit

**1 Timothy 4:1 "Now the Spirit speaketh expressly, that in the latter times some shall depart from the faith, giving heed to seducing spirits, and doctrines of devils;"**

**Job 22:21; "Acquaint now thyself with him, and be at peace: thereby good shall come unto thee."**

You must become very acquainted with the Spirit of God. He already indwells you. Jesus said, 'When he the Spirit of truth comes, he will guide you into all truth. He will not speak on his own; he will speak only what he hears, and he will tell you what is yet to come."(John 16:13). Paul in his second epistle to the Corinthian saints makes this great endeavor for every believer,

**2 Corinthians 13:14; "The grace of the Lord Jesus Christ, and the love of God, and the communion of the Holy Ghost, be with you all. Amen."**

Notice '...the communion of the Holy Spirit be with you all.' This is not just for pastors or people in the fivefold ministry offices. It is for all. The word 'communion' is the Greek word 'Koinonia' and it has a threefold meaning,

1- Relationship

2- Fellowship

3- Partnership

When you were born again, you entered into a relationship with the Holy Spirit as he now indwells you. However you need to learn to fellowship with him in order to have a successful partnership with him. The root of Koinonia means to communicate and share in the same realities, properties or even problems with another person. He is interested in solving your problem. I want to take you on a journey to know the voice of the Holy Spirit. I will also add some of my life's experiences to show you how God has led me and is still leading me. I believe these side stories will be of great value to you. They were to me! You must be totally convinced that the Holy Spirit wants to speak to you today. This is not just for pastors or people in the ministry, but for you also.

The voice of God is the key to breakthrough in life. It is your way out of complicated situations. You must understand that whatever is troubling you is not troubling God. Whatever is causing you to have sleepless nights and being fretful is not disturbing God in the least. Why? Because he knows what to do about your problem! The reason you are disturbed and worried is because you do not know what God knows. If you knew what God knew, you would be just like him, 'cool and collected'. Let me make this clear to you, although it is every believer's right to have access to the voice of God, it does not come cheaply. What I hope you will learn in this book is that hearing from God is a learned skill.

# CHAPTER 2

# TRUST GOD FOR DIRECTION

**Ecclesiastes 10:10; "If the iron be blunt, and he does not whet the edge, then must he put to more strength: <u>but wisdom is profitable to direct</u>."**

It is very clear from the Scriptures and life that directions and decisions have a major impact upon our lives. Many have endeavored to find happiness and success in life by relying upon their own power and mental faculties to lead them forward, only to realize that they were limited and hit the proverbial brick wall, from which they are yet to recover.

Receiving direction from God is very crucial to your success in life. In today's modern church where so many flippantly go around and declare, "The Lord told me this and the Lord told me that...", which when you examine, ninety nine percent of the time is nonsense and stupidity. They use this phraseology so that nobody can question them, and to get their own way.

Most of the time you can tell it is not the voice of God they heard but they heeded the voice of rebellion, as whatever they are saying and doing is in total violation to the Holy Scriptures and the character of God. Isn't it amazing that most people only hear God when it comes to leaving a church especially if they have been corrected by the pastor. It is astonishing how they can hear God to leave a church but can *never* hear God when it comes to any of their life's situations.

The voice of God is your access to victory. It is your way out of insurmountable problems. As I already mentioned, every believer has the divine right to have access to the voice of God, but it does not come cheaply. ***Hearing from God is a learned skill.*** Now because many have not learnt and developed this skill, they have resorted to fleecing for direction. 'Putting out a fleece' as it is often expressed, involves seeking God's will or direction through a sign. For example someone says, "Lord, if this is really you then let my phone ring three times or let a blue bus come in front of me." You may think that this sounds absurd but there are literally millions of believers who live their lives in this order. That is not God's best! Satan can easily manipulate and deceive people with fleeces.

Many have fallen in his trap. **God's best is for his people to be led by the Spirit.** Some have argued, 'If it was good enough for Gideon, it is good enough for me.' The 'fleece' concept is based on Gideon who was one of the leaders that God raised up to deliver Israel from the Midianites. The Angel of the Lord appeared to him and gave him specific instructions. But before Gideon would commit himself to battle, he wanted to make sure that God was going to give Israel the victory and he started his fleecings,

Judges 6:36-40; "Then Gideon said to God, "If you are truly going to use me to rescue Israel as you promised, prove it to me in this way. I will put a wool fleece on the threshing floor tonight. If the fleece is wet with dew in the morning but the ground is dry, then I will know that you are going to help me rescue Israel as you promised." And that is just what happened. When Gideon got up early the next morning, he squeezed the fleece and wrung out a whole bowlful of water. Then Gideon said to God, "Please don't be angry with me, but let me make one more request. Let me use the fleece for one more test. This time let the fleece remain dry while the ground around it is wet with dew." So that night God did as Gideon asked. The fleece was dry in the morning, but the ground was covered with dew."

As we study and scrutinize this event  there will be a couple of things to note:

Firstly, Gideon did not put the fleece in order to discover the will of God. He already knew that from the angel who specifically told him what must transpire. Gideon knew what God wanted him to do nevertheless he went ahead with the fleece.

Secondly, the fleece was a sign of unbelief. The Lord Jesus himself had some strong words for those who ask for signs, 'Then certain of the scribes and of the Pharisees answered, saying, *Master, we would see a sign from thee.* But he answered and said unto them, *An evil and adulterous generation seeketh after a sign;* and there shall no sign be given to it, but the sign of the prophet Jonas:" (Matthew 12:38,39) Asking for signs, typifies today's believers who walk by sight rather than walking by faith. Gideon had already received a miraculous sign from God pointing him to victory and deliverance for Israel.

Nevertheless Gideon doubted even after the angel of the Lord appeared to him, he wanted one sign after another sign. Gideon knew God's will but didn't believe it. 'Putting out a fleece' was an act of faithlessness because Gideon didn't trust that God would do what He had already promised. He wanted more signs when an angel speaking to him should have been enough sign already. Jesus told us, *'Blessed are they that have not seen, and yet have believed.'*(John 20:29) Many years ago Kenneth Hagin taught the church world, 'Fleeces are an Old Covenant method of guidance used by spiritually dead people. We have a better guide, the living Spirit of God in direct communion with our spirit." You are not spiritually dead but alive in Christ by the Holy Ghost. So let me say this categorically, "Fleecing is not the way God wants to give you direction." You have to press into God in order to hear him. Luke 5:1; "And it came to pass, that, as the people pressed upon him to hear the word of God, he stood by the lake of Gennesaret,…" Allow me to re-emphasize this point in your mind. Although it is the birthright of every believer to receive direction from the mouth of God, yet it will not come cheaply nor with a flippant or nonchalant attitude. You must learn to press for his voice to direct your steps

> *It is the birthright of every believer to receive direction from the mouth of God, yet it does not come cheaply nor with a flippant or nonchalant attitude.*

## Defining Direction

Direction is defined in the dictionary as

* A course along which someone or something moves

* A point to or from which a person or thing moves.

* The management or guidance of someone or something

Receiving direction from above is to receive heaven's idea concerning your life and future. Divine direction is direction from God. It is following the course, path and plan of God for your life, career and ministry. Direction from Above is absolutely critical for your breakthrough and victory in life. God has a specific plan and path for your life. Direction from above is basically the Holy Ghost communicating the plan and mind of God to our spirits.

*Direction from above is following the course, path and plan of God for your life, career and ministry*

It is pivotal for you to discover this plan and be led by his voice. Isaiah revealed the great benefit of being led by God, **"And they thirsted not when he led them through the deserts: he caused the waters to flow out of the rock for them:** he clave the rock also, and the waters gushed out." (Isaiah 48:21). As long as God is leading you, it does not matter if it looks like the wilderness, you will not thirst and go hungry. Israel is proof of that! Jeremiah gives us a great clue concerning the path that God led them out of, "Thus saith the LORD, What iniquity have your fathers found in me, that they are gone far from me, and have walked after vanity, and are become vain? Neither said they, Where is the Lord that brought us up out of the land of Egypt, that led us through the wilderness, through a land of deserts and pits, through a land of drought, and of the shadow of death, through a land that no man passed through, and where no man dwelt?" (Jeremiah 2:5, 6)

Notice it was a land of pits and death through which no man could pass and yet God led them safely and sustained them abundantly. In fact Moses tells us even more concerning this wilderness, 'God led thee through that great and terrible wilderness, wherein were **fiery serpents, and scorpions, and drought, where there was no water;** who brought thee forth water out of the rock of flint.' (Deuteronomy 8:15).

As long as God led them, they escaped serpents and

scorpions. How does this apply to us today? These were types of demonic spirits waiting to pounce upon God's people but could not do so as God was leading them. The same will be your portion!

Every devil in the way, waiting to pounce on you will not find you as you follow the leadings of God. Another great example of someone who was fed and prospered for following divine direction is Isaac. When there was a great famine, Isaac chose to follow the direction of God when everything within him was screaming to leave Gerar and go down to Egypt for help. What was the end result? He became so blessed and was the envy of his enemies.

> Genesis 26:12-14; "Then Isaac sowed in that land, and <u>received in the same year an hundredfold: and the LORD blessed him</u>.
>
> And the man waxed great, and went forward, and grew until he became very great:
>
> For he had possession of flocks, and possession of herds, and great store of servants: and the Philistines envied him."

You have to learn to trust God with everything in your life, career and ministry. This is your first step to experience the bountiful supplies of God.

> Proverbs 3:5-7; "Trust in the LORD with all thine heart; and lean not unto thine own understanding. In all thy ways acknowledge him, and he shall direct thy paths."
>
> Proverbs 3:5-7; "Trust in the LORD with all your heart; do not depend on your own understanding. Seek his will in all you do, and he will direct your paths. Don't be impressed with your own wisdom. Instead, fear the LORD and turn your back on evil." New Living

**Translation**

You must believe that God wants to guide and lead you. If you are not convinced of this fact then you will take matters into your own hands which often brings catastrophic results. Living life without God's direction and wisdom is like a hamster spinning a wheel. There is a lot of movement but you are not going anywhere.

Our Lord Jesus walked in constant victory because he only did what his Father beckoned him to do. Even the Lord himself uttered, "I can of my own self do nothing: as I hear, I judge: and my judgment is just; because I seek not my own will, but the will of the Father which has sent me." That was the key to a breakthrough life. You cannot make it by yourself. This revelation impacted the great Prophet Jeremiah when he uttered,

> **Jeremiah 10:23; "O Lord, I know that the way of man is not in himself: <u>it is not in man that walketh to direct his steps.</u>"**

There are men and women today who insist on being a self- made person. In effect what they are saying is, 'I don't need God, I can find my way myself.' A believer must never reason like that. Rather we should heed the advice of King Solomon,

> **Proverbs 3:5-7; "Trust God from the bottom of your heart; <u>don't try to figure out everything on your own</u>. Listen for God's voice in everything you do, everywhere you go; he's the one who will keep you on track. <u>Don't assume that you know it all. Run to God</u>..." The Message Translation**

## *Why is direction from above imperative to the believer?*

### *To be on the right track

Man cannot lead himself. Don't assume you know it all. Run to God. You see as human beings we are limited in our capacity. We can only see what is in front of us. The Message Translation aptly pens it, 'Don't assume you know it all. Run to God.' When we make decisions, we do so based upon our knowledge, education level and experience. However we do not know and do not foresee what can happen in the middle of the situation or what the end result might turn out to be.

However, Our Lord Jesus Christ is known as the First and the Last, the Beginning and the End. When we make a decision or take a direction in which he has led us, he already knew what was in the middle and the end. You do not know and cannot see the pitfalls, traps and snares that satan has planted but the Lord does.

> Proverbs 14:12; "There is a way which seemeth right unto a man, but the end thereof are the ways of death."

> Proverbs 16:25; "There is a way which seemeth right unto a man, but the end thereof are the ways of death."

How many times have you made a decision that at the beginning you thought was the real deal only to discover it was a major mistake later on? All of us have experienced this dilemma! At the start it all looked good but the end was devastating.

### *To avoid pitfalls and destruction

God is forever trying to get our attention so that we can avoid pain, heartache and financial loss. The primary reason why we experience destruction is because our ears are not tuned in to the voice of God. Your problem is not that God is not speaking, it is that you cannot hear God. HE HAS NO SPEAKING PROBLEM, YOU HAVE A HEARING PROBLEM.

> Job 33:14-18; "For God speaketh once, yea twice, yet man perceiveth it not. In a dream, in a vision of the night, when deep sleep falleth upon men, in slumberings upon the bed; Then he openeth the ears of men, and sealeth their instruction, That he may withdraw man from his purpose, and hide pride from man. He keepth back his soul from the pit, and his life from perishing by the sword."

> Proverbs 14:12; "Some people think they are doing right, but in the end it leads to death." New Century Version

## *To avoid stagnation in life

God hates stagnation. You must hate stagnation. Israel was trained by God to follow the pillar of cloud by day and pillar of fire by night to avoid camping in a place where God does not want you to camp. Many have overstayed in what was meant to be a transitional period and became stagnant and barren in life. Things turn sour when you stay in a place where God did not command you to stay. The great prophet Micah opens this truth to us,

> Micah 2:10; "Get up and leave. This is not your place of rest anymore. You have made this place unclean, and it is doomed to destruction." New Century Version

## *To do that which is right in God's eyes.

When one has not accessed wisdom from above to move forward in life then one is just doing what is right in one's own eyes. The books of Kings and Chronicles give us a chronological and systematic documentation of men and women who did that which was right or evil in the sight of God. All without exception reaped consequences. He who did right in the eyes of God reaped beneficiary consequences and those who did evil reaped affliction, blight, scourge, plague or dire situations.

From today I want you to be assured in this fact that the Lord wants to lead and guide you. Here is a commitment to you from the mouth of the Master.

> Isaiah 48:16, 17; "Come ye near unto me, hear ye this; I have not spoken in secret from the beginning; from the time that it was, there am I: and now the Lord GOD, and his Spirit, hath sent me.
>
> <u>Thus saith the LORD, thy Redeemer, the Holy One of Israel; I am the LORD thy God which leadeth thee by the way that thou shouldest go.</u>
>
> O that thou hadst hearkened to my commandments! then had thy peace been as a river, and thy righteousness as the waves of the sea: Thy seed also had been as the sand, and the offspring of thy bowels like the gravel thereof; his name should not have been cut off nor destroyed from before me.
>
> Go ye forth of Babylon, flee ye from the Chaldeans, with a voice of singing declare ye, tell this, utter it even to the end of the earth; say ye, The LORD hath redeemed his servant Jacob.
>
> And they thirsted not when he had them through the deserts: he caused the waters to flow out of the rock for them: he clave the rock also, and the waters gushed out.
>
> There is no peace, saith the LORD, unto the wicked."

Here are some gleanings I want you to get from this passage:

**1. Jesus has pledged and is unwavering in his commitment to lead you**

\* **'I am the Lord thy God, thy Redeemer'** This is your Savior, Messiah, Redeemer and Lord addressing you. This is an irrevocable pledge from the mouth of the Redeemer, "I am the Lord thy God, thy redeemer...who leadeth thee by the way thou should go..." From now on, settle it in your spirit that you do not have to leave or enter any endeavor without the leading of God. It is your right and privilege to be led by him.

**2. His direction alone will lead you to profit**

*'I am the LORD thy God which teacheth thee to profit, which leadeth thee by the way that thou shouldest go.'* Jesus, your Redeemer is totally committed to leading you to which way you should go. This implies He knows the right way. Remember He is the way, the truth and the life. It is when we go the right way that we will experience peace, profit and prosperity. You can have the same testimony that Uzziah had,

> 2 Chronicles 26:4,5; "And he did that which was right in the sight of the LORD, according to all that his father Amaziah did. And he <u>sought God</u> in the days of Zechariah, who had understanding in the visions of God: and <u>as long as he sought the LORD, God made him to prosper.</u>"

*'As long as he sought the LORD, God made him to prosper.'* May this become your portion and reality in life! As humans, we have short-sightedness and our vision is limited. Only God who has a panoramic view can tell you the whole picture. Profit is the proof that you have heeded his direction and loss is the proof you have missed his leading.

**3. Your hearkening and obedience are pivotal to your safety. They will trigger peace and prosperity**

*'O that thou hadst hearkened to my commandments! then had thy peace been as a river, and thy righteousness as the*

*waves of the sea.'* If you would only listen to Jesus then you will experience peace, which is the Hebrew word 'Shalom' meaning 'nothing missing, nothing broken'. Following God's voice will bring you to a place of no destruction. One bad decision can affect your life as well as your goods. Paul knew this as he was a man sensitive to the voice of God.

> Acts 27:10; "And said unto them, Sirs, I perceive that this voyage will be with hurt and much damage, not only of the lading and ship, but also of our lives."

**4. Your ability to hear and obey his instruction will protect your generation**

*'Thy seed also had been as the sand, and the offspring of thy bowels like the gravel thereof; his name should not have been cut off nor destroyed from before me.'*

Following the voice of Jesus will protect your children, they would grow healthily and not be cut off or suffer premature death. Your decision to lean on the leading of God will not only affect your betterment but your future generations.

**5. No recession, inflation and economic downturn will affect you**

*'And they thirsted not when he led them through the deserts.'* As long as you follow the Lord, you will not experience thirst. Let that be you confession today, 'I will not thirst as long as I follow the voice of my Redeemer.' See what happened when God's people were led by God's man, Moses.

> Deuteronomy 29:5; "And I have led you forty years in the wilderness: your clothes are not waxen old upon you, and thy shoe is not waxen old upon thy foot."

As you make the decision to follow the leading of God, there will no more be loss or wastage in your life.

CHAPTER 3

# FOL-LOWING DIRECTION FROM ABOVE

You must realize that the will and plan of God for your life is a path already prepared, that you must discover. For you to be truly successful in life, it behooves you to discover that chosen path that God already has for you. The Psalmist calls it the path of life, 'Thou wilt shew me the path of life: in thy presence is fulness of joy; at thy right hand there are pleasures for evermore.' (Psalm 16:11) The Prophet Jeremiah called it the old path,

Jeremiah 6:16; *"Thus saith the LORD, Stand ye in the ways, and see, and ask for the old paths, where is the good way, and walk therein, and ye shall find rest for your souls."*

*The will and plan of God for your life is a path already prepared, that you must discover*

There is safety, prosperity and victory when you discover that secret path. Unfortunately many believers never take the time to discover that plan that God has for them. Job illuminates our minds further with this revelation,

**Job 28: 7, 8; "There is a path which no fowl knoweth, and which the vulture's eye hath not seen: The lion's whelps have not trodden it, nor the fierce lion passed by it."**

It is your responsibility to discover that path. Your major task in life is to always locate the plan and direction in which God wants you to move. It is not going to drop into your lap automatically. See the wisdom of Solomon as he articulates this truth, 'It is the glory of God to conceal a thing: but the honor of kings is to search out a matter.' It will be to your honor to search out God's private plans for your life. No one can do that for you. There comes a time in your life where you need to step up and stop running around looking for a man to prophesy on you. The Holy Spirit is right there with you and he wants to talk to you. Here is what I want you to grasp,

> Proverbs 3:5-7; "Trust God from the bottom of your heart; don't try to figure out everything on your own. <u>Listen for God's voice in everything you do, everywhere you go; he's the one who will keep you on track.</u> Don't assume that you know it all. Run to God! Run from evil!" The Message Translation.

**1. "Listen for God's voice in everything you do, everywhere you go. He's the one who will keep you on track."**

From today, make the quality decision that you will follow God in everything that you do and everywhere that you go. Those who know the voice of God will eliminate frustration, worry, fear, doubt and anxiety out of their lives. Those who do not know how to discern the voice of God to receive direction will be victims of circumstances.

> Proverbs 29:18; "Where there is no vision, the people perish."

> Proverbs 29:18; "When people do not accept divine guidance, they run wild." New Living Translation

When you do not have direction from above then you will

run wildly in life. Lack of 'direction from above' will make you a wandering generality rather than a meaningful specific, to borrow a great quote from Zig Ziglar. Take the time to be quiet before the Lord. If you have to fast and pray and set yourself aside to hear him, then DO IT. Accessing the voice of God will not come cheaply. Hearing from God is a learned skill.

**2. Those who made their marks in the earth were those who had received instruction from above and applied it.**

The whole bible gives us a litany of them but here are two prime examples:-

## *Paul*

Acts 9:6; "And he trembling and astonished said, Lord, what wilt thou have me to do? And the Lord said unto him, Arise, and go into the city, and it shall be told thee what thou must do."

## *David*

2 Samuel 5:17-20; "But when the Philistines heard that they had anointed David king over Israel, all the Philistines came up to seek David; and David heard of it, and went down to the strong hold.

The Philistines also came and spread themselves in the valley of Rephaim. And David enquired of the LORD, saying, Shall I go up to the Philistine? Wilt thou deliver them into mine hand? And the LORD said unto David, Go up: for I will doubtless deliver the Philistines into thine hand.

And David came to Baalperazim, and David smote them there, and said, the LORD hath broken forth upon mine enemies before me, as the breach of waters. Therefore he called the name of that place Baalperazim."

**Baalperazim** simply means "Lord of the Breakthrough".

Every breakthrough that you will experience in life will be traced back to the voice of God. I love the fact that breakthroughs are associated with following God. The word 'breakthrough' means,

*Every breakthrough that you will experience in life will be traced back to the voice of God*

'A significant and dramatic overcoming of a perceived obstacle, allowing the completion of a process'.

'A major advancement'

' A situation where an offensive force has broken through an enemy defensive line'

' An important discovery'

This is what I see for you today! As you follow God's leading, you are about to have a major advancement in your life, career and ministry. You are breaking through an enemy's defensive line to get to your Promised Land. There is coming into your life a significant and dramatic overcoming of a major obstacle allowing you to complete your assignment. Rejoice! Your days of being overlooked, passed over and rejected are over! You are about to be discovered and be in the limelight. This is your season, this is your day! Take it as God's word for you today!

CHAPTER 4

# THE TWO PREDOMINANT WAYS TO RECEIVE DIRECTION

**Job 33:14-19; "For God speaketh once, yea twice, yet man perceiveth it not. In a dream, in a vision of the night, when deep sleep falleth upon men, in slumberings upon the bed; Then he openeth the ears of men, and sealeth their instruction, That he may withdraw man from his purpose, and hide pride from man. He keepeth back his soul from the pit, and his life from perishing by the sword."**

How will I receive direction from above? God can lead and direct in many ways. The Bible unveils to us a myriad of avenues that God communicates with his people. Here are some of the ways that God directs and communicates,

*Vision

*Dream

*Fivefold ministries

*Audible voice

*Angelic visitation

*Gifts of the Spirit

*Prophetic utterance

*Voice in your ear

All the above are important and extremely valuable. All of them have played their roles in the Scriptures and will probably play a part in your life at some point as the Spirit wills. God used dreams, visions, prophets, seers and angels in the Old Testament as well as the New Testament. People love these because they are spectacular in nature. However, for us New Testament believers, the two predominant ways that God wants to leads us are through,

**A. The Voice of the Word**

**B. The Voice of the Spirit**

*You can miss the supernatural by looking and focusing on the spectacular.*

You can miss the supernatural by looking and focusing on the spectacular. Many times the voice of God is not spectacular but a still small voice or an impression. So let us examine the voice of the Word and the voice of the Spirit.

## *The voice of the Word*

The Bible is God speaking to you. Many years ago, I saw Kenneth Copeland holding up his bible and say, 'This is not just a book, this is God speaking to you.' That hit me hard! I grasped and understood it. Brother Copeland also said, 'One Word from God can change your life forever.' I believe that with all my heart and fiber of my being. Your relationship with God can only be as deep as your fellowship with His Word. The Word is heaven's communication to earthly children. It is heavenly thoughts that will cause you to rise above the earthly circumstances. Now, you need to understand that the Bible gives us the general parameters by which we live our lives. Therefore general guidance comes from the Written Word. A believer must be conversant with the Word and allow it to order his general steps. By the term 'general' I mean the common or standard will that God has for all his saints. For example, it is through the bible that you discover that God wants you healed and filled with the Holy Spirit. That's for everybody. It is through the bible that you discover that fruitfulness and the abundant life are available to the believer. Everyone who is born again can partake of the promises of the Written Word.

*The Bible gives us the general parameters by which we live our lives. Therefore general guidance comes from the Written Word*

The more you meditate on God's word, the more it will speak to you and keep you safe and straight. The Psalmist said, *"Wherewithal shall a young man cleanse his way? By taking heed thereto according to thy word. With my whole heart have I sought thee: O let me not wander from thy commandments. Thy word have I hid in mine heart, that I might not sin against thee."* (Psalm 119:9-11) God's Word is our escape from the traps of our enemies and *our guide in life. Peter calls the Scriptures 'a more sure word of prophecy'*(2 Peter 1:19) and Paul says *'it makes you wise unto salvation.'*(2 Timothy 3:15). Meditating upon the Word will trigger profit in all areas of your life.

The Written Word is the Logos and the Quickened or Spoken Word is Rhema. You see God's Word was first spoken so that it can be written and it was written in order that when you meditate upon it, it will quicken and speak to you. It will speak to you concerning your marriage, your health, your business and every area of your life. Allow the Word to shape your life. How many times has this happened to you? While you were reading your bible, all of a sudden a Scripture jumps out at you. You've read it many times before and that Scripture has been there all the time but that particular day it jumped at you and a revelation hit you. It has happened to me numerous times and I shouted, 'Yea! That's it! This is my answer!' What just happened there?

Well, the Holy Spirit just ignited that Word and opened the eyes of your spirit. This verse now speaks to you on a heart level rather than just head-knowledge. It is now the 'how to' of fixing the problem you are going through. It is now revelation for application to become the solution to the situation. I remember as a young believer how flabbergasted I was when every time I opened my bible it would seem like the verses were talking to me about the issue at hand. I know you have experienced the same. It gave me a heavenly response to my earthly predicament. It is still the same today! It will do the same for you, if you first come before God humbly and in prayer.

The voice of the Word will deliver you. Sometimes you will be in a situation and all of a sudden a Scripture will come alive in your spirit and mind. What is that? That's a quickened Word! That's the Word that God has given you for the moment to deal with your situation. Solomon said these words, *'My son attend unto my words, incline your ears unto my sayings...'* (Proverbs 4:20) Here is a great truth to grasp, **'When you incline your ears to attend to his Words, then they will become sayings to your life.'** Therefore your meditation of the Word is without doubt the most noble task that you ever endeavor to tap into. The Bible is the wisdom of God to direct, on pages. The Word trains a child and trains the man of God.

2 Timothy 3:14-17; "But continue thou in the things which

thou hast learned and hast been assured of, knowing of whom thou hast learned them; And that from a child thou hast known the holy scriptures, which are able to make thee wise unto salvation through faith which is in Christ Jesus. All scripture is given by inspiration of God, and is profitable for doctrine, for reproof, for correction, for instruction in righteousness: That the man of God may be perfect, thoroughly furnished unto all good works."

**Proverbs 22:6; "Train up a child in the way he should go: and when he is old, he will not depart from it."**

Your destiny is in the word. The Lord Jesus found himself in the book of Isaiah. It will behoove you to search the scriptures to discover yourself and your God-given destiny.

*When you incline your ears to attend to his Words, then they will become sayings to your life*

**Isaiah 34:16" Seek ye out of the book of the Lord, and read: no one of these shall fail, none shall want her mate: for my mouth it hath commanded, and his spirit it hath gathered them.**

Here is a quote from an anonymous author concerning the bible that I believe will be of tremendous help to you and I,

"This book is the mind of God, the state of man, the way of salvation, the doom of sinners and the happiness of believers. Its doctrines are holy, its precepts are binding; its histories are true and its decisions are immutable. Read it to be wise, believe it to be safe, practice it to be holy.  It contains light to direct you, food to support you and comfort to cheer you. It is the traveler's map, the pilgrim's staff, the pilot's compass, the soldier's sword and the Christian's Character.

Here paradise is restored, heaven opened, and the gates of hell disclosed.  Christ is its grand subject, our good its design and the glory of God its end. It should fill the memory, rule the heart, and guide the feet. Read it slowly, frequently, and prayerfully. It is a mine of wealth, a paradise of glory and a river of pleasure. Follow its precepts and it will lead you to Calvary, to the empty tomb, to a resurrected life in Christ and yes, to glory itself, for eternity"

## Important Point

One very important point I want to make to you is to make sure you go to a church that teaches the Word of God. If you were to ask the average believer,'Why do you go to this church?' One of the most common replies that you will hear is 'Well, it's close to my house.' Now as convenient as that might be, it is not a good reason. That is like me saying, 'I eat out of this garbage can because it is close to me.' I do not go to my church because it is close to me. I go to church where I get fed the Word of God. It may not have the latest technology or cinema chairs but if the pastor teaches the Word, then this is where I will go.

The voice of the Word will emanate from the man or woman of God. I realize that today people go to a church that provides life's comfort such as nice chairs, huge cinema screen, smoke machine, dimming lights during praise and worship etc and that's all great. However my quest in church attendance is to receive the Word. I don't go to church because I'm a fan of the pastor or because he makes me laugh. Nothing wrong with laughter but I am after the Word. I want a teaching priest for a pastor not a motivational speaker and not a comedian.

> **2 Chronicles 15:3; "Now for a long season Israel hath been without the true God, and without a teaching priest, and without law."**

Notice these three things,

#1. Without the true God

#2. Without a teaching priest

#3. Without law

You need to go to a church that teaches the uncompromised Word of God. You need a pastor who is Scripturally correct rather than being politically correct and gives you the mind of God each week. The Word is God speaking to you!

## *The Voice of the Spirit*

If the Bible gives us the general parameters by which we measure our lives and live, then the voice of the Spirit addresses the specific framework of our lives. You see, all of us have generalities in our lives but we also have some important specifics. The Bible gives the general will or guidance of God for every believer irrespective of color, race and age. Whereas the voice of the Spirit gives the specific guidance or direction for you. The voice of the Spirit is specific

> *The voice of the Spirit gives the specific guidance or direction for you. The voice of the Spirit is specific divine direction to you*

divine direction to you! It addresses your life in the present and the future.

'Where are you supposed to move to?'

'Who am I to marry?'

'What am I supposed to do with my life and career?'

'What is my next step?'

'Do I plant the church in Los Angeles or Washington DC?'

One thing is for sure, you will not find Los Angeles mentioned in the Bible. You certainly won't find, 'Thou shall marry Peggy Sue ' or whatever person you are interested in, in the Bible. Many other questions need specific direction and you obtain these specific instructions by knowing the voice of the Spirit. Jesus told us that the Holy Spirit will guide and lead us as well as showing us things to come. How will he do this? ___*The Holy Spirit will lead you by your spirit.*___ This is an important fact that you must grasp. He does not lead you through your head or emotions but through your born again spirit.

Let me reiterate this fact again, ___*The Holy Spirit will lead you by your spirit.*___

> **Proverbs 20:27; "The spirit of man is the candle of the Lord, searching all the inward parts of the belly."**

> **Romans 8: 10-16; "But ye are not in the flesh, but in the Spirit, *if so be that the Spirit of God dwell in you.* Now if any man have not the Spirit of Christ, he is none of his.**

And if Christ be in you, the body is dead because of sin; but the Spirit is life because of righteousness. *But if the Spirit of him that raised up Jesus from the dead dwell in you,* he that raised up Christ from the dead shall also quicken your mortal bodies by *his Spirit that dwelleth in you.* Therefore, brethren, we are debtors, not to the flesh, to live after the flesh. For if ye live after the flesh, ye shall die: but if ye through the Spirit do mortify the deeds of the body, ye shall live. *For as many as are led by the Spirit of God, they are the sons of God.* For ye have not received the spirit of bondage again to fear; but ye have received the Spirit of adoption, whereby we cry, Abba, Father. *The Spirit itself beareth witness with our spirit,* that we are the children of God..."

*The Holy Spirit will lead you by your spirit. He does not lead you through your head or emotions but through your born again spirit*

34

In the space of a few verses, three times Paul reminds the believer that he is indwelt by the Holy Spirit. Then because we are indwelt by the Spirit, we are to be led by the Spirit. He does so by bearing witness with our spirit. Pay attention to these words, *'The Spirit itself beareth witness with our spirit.'* Now connect that with Solomon's revelation, 'The Spirit of man is the candle of the Lord.' A better translation of this verse is, 'The Spirit of man is the lamp of the Lord.' A lamp or a candle was used in olden days as a form of enlightenment for the night. There was no General Electric in the olden days, therefore at night it would be pitch dark. The only guidance they would receive to properly maneuver the right movement is the candle, the wooden torch or a lamp. They did so in order to avoid holes and snakes in the dark.

*God will light you up and guide you from your spirit, the inner man*

Psalms 18:28; "For You will light my lamp; The Lord my God will enlighten my darkness."

Proverbs 20:27; "The spirit of man is the candle of the Lord, searching all the inward parts of the belly."

Your spirit is the lamp or candle of the Lord and the Psalmist says that God will light your lamp. That's your spirit. He will light you up from your spirit. Born-again believers have the Holy Spirit living in them to lead and guide them. The Holy Spirit will guide you from your spirit man. Therefore there is no need for you, the believer, to look for direction and guidance from outside forces such as a fleece, a word, an open door or a closed door. The Holy Spirit will direct you from your inner man.

CHAPTER 5

# THE HOLY SPIRIT AND THE HUMAN SPIRIT

Let this truth be wrapped around your mind, 'God will lead you by your spirit'. The Holy Spirit, who is our counsellor and helper will bear witness with your spirit. Understanding the 'witness of the spirit' is crucial to you receiving direction to move forward in life. I want to submit to you that if you do not understand the inward witness of the Spirit, then you will struggle to be led by God. Paul tells us, *'For as many as are led by the Spirit of God, they are the sons of God. For ye have not received the spirit of bondage again to fear; but ye have received the Spirit of adoption, whereby we cry, Abba, Father. The Spirit itself beareth witness with our spirit, that we are the children of God.'(Romans 8:13-16)*

Now I want us to look at the connection of the Holy Spirit and the human spirit for direction and guidance. These are the words of Jesus, 'But when he, the Spirit of truth, comes, he will guide you into all truth. He will not speak on his own; he will speak only what he hears, and he will tell you what is yet to come.' (John 16:13) The Holy Spirit will tell you what is yet to come. One Bible translates this verse as, *'He will show you the future'*. That is fantastic! You don't ever need to be in the dark with the Holy Spirit within you. The two important particulars of receiving direction are the Holy Spirit and the human spirit. You need to understand the connection. Let us briefly look at them respectively.

## The Holy Spirit

First, let's have a condensed but concise look at some characteristics of the Holy Spirit.

**Who is He?**

**How does He work?**

What are his likes and dislikes? By answering these questions you will get  to know Him better thereby enabling you to grasp how He is going to lead you.

## Who is the Holy Spirit?

He is the third person of the Godhead. He is Deity and He is just as much God as Jesus or the Father are. He is not an 'it', He is a person. He was there at Creation. He was there for the Incarnation of Christ and in the Resurrection, he raised Jesus from the dead. He is known as the Holy Spirit. Therefore He is not going to direct or guide you to do something unholy. The Holy Spirit always works in agreement with the Word. His leadings will never violate the Scriptures. Jesus told us that the Scripture cannot be broken.  The Holy Spirit is a gentleman. He never pushes to have his way. In the Scripture he is likened to a dove, fire, wind, a river and oil. He does not push! God said, 'My Spirit will not always strive with man...'(Genesis 6:3) The Holy Spirit does not fight to have his way. He does not like to be lied to as Ananias and Sapphira did. He can also be quenched and grieved as a person. He has gifts. The Holy Spirit is God. He speaks and He leads therefore he does not force.

## The Human spirit

First of all, understand that man is a tripartite being consisting of spirit, soul and body as revealed by Paul(1 Thessalonians 5:23) You do not have a spirit, you are a spirit. You are one because man is created in the image of God and Jesus said, 'God is a spirit.'(John 4:24) Man is a spirit, he has a soul and lives in a physical body. The real person is the spirit man. James lets us know that the body needs the spirit to be alive but the spirit is active without the body(James 2:26).

When you were born again, your spirit was recreated and became a new creature in Christ Jesus. It is your spirit man that was saved. Your soul is being saved as you renew your mind to the Word and your body will be saved eventually to take on immortality. A mind that is not renewed with the Word of God will lead you to do wrong things and to obey wrong voices. Paul says a carnal mind is enmity against God. Since it is your spirit that is recreated and born again, the Holy Spirit will guide you from this base.

Your spirit is the base of operation from which the Holy Spirit will direct and guide you. Therefore guidance is from

*Your spirit is the base of operation from which the Holy Spirit will direct and guide you. Therefore guidance is from the inside*

the inside. He does not direct from your soul as it cannot be trusted since it is being saved gradually. He will not guide you from the body. Solomon said, 'The spirit of man is the candle of the Lord.' He did not say, "The body of man is the candle of the Lord," nor does it say, "The mind of man is the candle of the Lord." Your answer is in your spirit.

> **Proverbs 20:5; "Counsel in the heart of man is like deep water; but a man of understanding will draw it out."**

Notice these words, 'Counsel in the heart of man..' It is in your spirit. The heart of man is not referring to his physical organ known as the heart but to the core of man, which is the spirit. The Holy Spirit is residing within your spirit man. Notice it says,' Counsel in the heart of man is like deep water', you have to learn to draw it out. Now connect these three verses,

> **Proverbs 20:5; "Counsel in the heart of man is like deep water; but <u>a man of understanding</u> will draw it out."**

> **Job 32:8; "But it is the spirit in a man, the <u>breath of the Almighty, that gives him understanding.</u>"**

> **Proverbs 3:5,6; "Trust in the Lord with all thine heart; and <u>lean not unto thine own understanding.</u> In all thy ways acknowledge him, and he shall direct thy paths."**

You won't draw it out from your mental faculties but from your spirit. That is why Solomon says not to lean on your own understanding. The Holy Spirit in you knows all things that God has prepared for you. He knows everything about you. All the good things that God has already prepared for you, he knows them and he wants to reveal them to you through your spirit. For you to find out what God has prepared for you, you will have to discern them from your spirit. What you must realize is that right now within you are all the answers you will ever need. You do not have to look for a man to give you a word or run to a prophetic meeting. The mighty Holy Spirit in your spirit man is keen to give you the answers you are looking for,

> **1 Corinthians 2:7-16; "But as it is written, Eye hath not seen, nor ear heard, neither have entered into the heart**

of man, <u>the things which God hath prepared for them that love him. But God hath revealed them unto us by his Spirit:</u> for the Spirit searcheth all things, yea, the deep things of God. For what man knoweth the things of a man, save the spirit of man which is in him? even so the things of God knoweth no man, but the Spirit of God. Now we have received, not the spirit of the world, but the spirit which is of God; that we might know the things that are freely given to us of God. Which things also we speak, not in the words which man's wisdom teacheth, but which the Holy Ghost teacheth; comparing spiritual things with spiritual. But the natural man receiveth not the things of the Spirit of God: for they are foolishness unto him: neither can he know them, because they are spiritually discerned. But he that is spiritual judgeth all things, yet he himself is judged of no man. For who hath known the mind of the Lord, that he may instruct him? but we have the mind of Christ."

I want to end this chapter with this thought in your head that the Holy Spirit will guide you from your spirit. He leads from the inside and not the outside. Learn to follow the Holy Spirit from the inside as the children of Israel followed the cloud by day and the pillar of fire by night. When the cloud moved, they moved. When it stopped, they stopped. God trained them to follow the cloud. Train your spirit man to follow the leading and prompting of the Holy Spirit.

# CHAPTER 6

# THE VOICE OF THE SPIRIT AND THE INWARD WITNESS

How will you recognize the voice of the Spirit? How will you identify the leading of the Holy Spirit? How will you pick up what's inside your spirit. What are the signals that we are tapping into the voice of the Spirit or the inward witness of the Spirit. Over the years, people have learnt how to discern his directions and endeavor to explain and express the indications they had. Allow me to list some indications for you,

*Inward knowing

*Inward intuition

*Perception

*Still small voice

*A prompting

*A check in my spirit

*Peace

*Liberty in spirit

RECEIVING DIRECTION FROM ABOVE

\*Joy

\*Conscience

\*Green light or red light

\*Unrest in your spirit

\*Hunch

The inward witness of the Spirit within your spirit is the one major avenue whereby God leads us. It is imperative that we become sensitive to the voice of the Holy Spirit to guide us successfully in our future. Sometimes people have described it as a 'feeling of uneasiness' and at other times, 'I have a peace about it'. It is like having a green light in your spirit to move forward or a red light giving you a warning to stop. Some have described it as, 'I just know something within me'.

What is that? That's the voice of the Spirit communicating with you! It is pretty much like in the Old Testament with the Urim and Thummin. When the children of Israel needed guidance, apart from seeking a seer or prophet, they would seek it from the priest who then would see if the Urim and Thummin glows for them to go forward. Hence that's why the inward witness has been called a red or green light. When God leads you in a direction, you might feel an inexplicable desire in your spirit toward a particular thing that never grabbed your attention before.

There are things that your spirit knows by the Spirit of God that your head does not have a single clue about. Most of the time God uses a tiny voice or expression inside us to let us know when we're not on the right track. Some have referred to it as "the voice of peace." Whenever you sense a lack of peace in a situation, stop and don't proceed further. If you have a check in your spirit, stop and check it. Don't override it. As soon as you feel the peace has lifted, stop in your tracks. I don't care how incorrect it may look. Stop now or later the damage might be too much. Always follow the peace. I can tell you that I have failed at that and it cost me dearly.

## *London 2005*

I remember a business transaction that I should not have entered but overrode the inward witness and I lost thousands of dollars. In 2005, while there was still a big boom in real estate in England, I made some money on one of my properties. I was excited! Then I listened to one so-called property expert to invest in an apartment complex that would double my investment in twelve months. It all sounded good as they showed me all the charts and figures. Apparently it was a done deal! I was impressed as they showed me all the previous deals and how much money all the investors made. Who doesn't want to double their investments in twelve months? That's more than the bank will ever give. All along with all the figures flying around and looking at the profit margin, something inside of me, a little small voice was gnawing at me not to get involved.

However, my reasoning was, 'This is an opportunity not to be missed and plus the property developer invited me to be part of something that most people are not privy to.' Secondly the property developer was a pastor and a Christian. So this sounded like a great deal. My investment would cost the equivalent of $60,000 in British Pounds Sterling to receive $120,000 in twelve months meaning the summer of 2006. I ignored that lack of peace! I ignored that inward witness! I can still remember writing the check, how uneasy I felt but nevertheless I ruled it as fear and having cold feet. I justified it by saying, 'We all need to take a risk sometimes'. In reality it was the Spirit of God warning me not to proceed.

To my shame, I overruled and overrode this check in my spirit. You can guess the outcome. That particular company went bust and was declared bankrupt. I have not seen my investment. I had to ask the Lord for forgiveness.

I want to remind you that God has said, 'My Spirit will not always strive with man.' When I decided to go my own way, the Holy Spirit who is a gentleman stood back and let me have my own way. The Apostle Paul clearly said, "And let the peace of God rule in your hearts." The Amplified Version is really excellent and is an eye opener, *'Let the peace of God... act as Umpire continually ... deciding and settling with finality all questions that arise in your minds.'* (Colossians 3:15, Amplified Bible)

There is a reason you don't feel peace about a situation or a person. The Spirit of God is saying , 'No, that's not the right way or right person.' Many times believers overrule and override this inward witness to their own detriment.

Don't override the impressions in your spirit. As a believer, it is utterly important that you become acquainted with the Holy Spirit through praying in other tongues. This is how you develop sensitivity to his voice and sustain partnership with him. After you pray, listen for his peaceful voice and instruction. You will recognize his voice because it will instill peace, liberty and joy in you in the midst of adverse circumstance.

Learn to do it in small things first to make proof of it. Listen then act upon it. Listen, then implement the instructions and directions. That's how you develop and grow spiritually to become a giant in faith. As you do so, you will also be able to say, "As long as God leads me, I am not going to thirst."

**Proverbs 3:5-7; "Trust God from the bottom of your heart; don't try to figure out everything on your own. Listen for**

*Many times believers overrule and override their inward witness to their own detriment. Don't override the impressions in your spirit*

God's voice in everything you do, everywhere you go; he's the one who will keep you on track. Don't assume that you know it all. Run to God..."

# CHAPTER 7

# EXAMPLES OF LEADINGS FROM PAUL'S LIFE AND MY PERSONAL LIFE

I want to take you on a mini tour of the Apostle Paul's life, how he was led by the Holy Spirit. This man knew God and he received direction from above through several means.

- Paul heard the audible voice of Jesus on the road to Damascus as recorded in the book of Acts(Acts 9:3-6).
- Paul received direction and instruction through vision (Acts 9:12, Acts 16:9, 10, Acts 18:9)
- Paul received instruction from an angel (Acts 27:23-25)
- Paul received wisdom from above through prophetic decree (Acts 21:1-0-14)
- Paul received direction and instruction through revelations (2 Corinthians 12:1, Galatians 2:2)
- Paul received instruction through the inward witness(Romans 8:16)
- Paul had guidance from his conscience being the voice and witness of the spirit(Romans 9:1)
- Paul had perception operating through him (Acts 27)

It is through the Pauline epistles that we read of the indwelling of the Spirit; the leading of the Spirit; the inward witness of the Spirit; the peace that acts as an umpire settling every question; the grieving of the human spirit; the conscience to guide; prophecies; tongues and interpretations of tongues; the word of wisdom and the word of knowledge; discernment of spirits and angelic visitations. This man's writings revealed to us how he was constantly seeking to be led by the Spirit of God. Now, I want us to look at how Paul was warned of danger through the inward witness of the Holy Spirit. This man was so sharp in the spirit that he knew things that natural eyes and people who were experts did not foresee. He defied the logic of the specialists.

## *Paul's perception*

We see an important aspect of divine guidance in Acts 27 that delivered the Apostle Paul and a lot of people from a catastrophic situation. If Paul did not know the voice of God, he would have lost his own life and those around him. It is to your advantage to tap into the voice of God. The twenty seventh chapter of the book of Acts is a great chapter on the subject of being led by the Spirit and not the flesh or five physical sense realm.

> Acts 27:1-16; "And when it was determined that we should sail into Italy, they delivered Paul and certain other prisoners unto one named Julius, a centurion of Augustus' band.
>
> And entering into a ship of Adramyttium, we launched, meaning to sail by the coasts of Asia; one Aristarchus, a Macedonian of Thessalonica, being with us. And the next day we touched at Sidon. And Julius courteously entreated Paul, and gave him liberty to go unto his

friends to refresh himself. And when we had launched from thence, we sailed under Cyprus, because the winds were contrary. And when we had sailed over the sea of Cilicia and Pamphylia, we came to Myra, a city of Lycia. And there the centurion found a ship of Alexandria sailing into Italy; and he put us therein. And when we had sailed slowly many days, and scarce were come over against Cnidus, the wind not suffering us, we sailed under Crete, over against Salmone; And, hardly passing it, came unto a place which is called The fair havens; nigh whereunto was the city of Lasea.

Now when much time was spent, and when sailing was now dangerous, because the fast was now already past, <u>Paul admonished them, And said unto them, Sirs, I perceive that this voyage will be with hurt and much damage, not only of the lading and ship, but also of our lives. Nevertheless the centurion believed the master and the owner of the ship, more than those things which were spoken by Paul.</u> And because the haven was not commodious to winter in, the more part advised to depart thence also, if by any means they might attain to Phenice, and there to winter; which is an haven of Crete, and lieth toward the south west and north west. <u>And when the south wind blew softly, supposing that they had obtained their purpose, loosing thence, they sailed close by Crete.</u> *But not long after there arose against it a tempestuous wind, called Euroclydon.*

*And when the ship was caught, and could not bear up into the wind, we let her drive.*

And running under a certain island which is called Clauda, we had much work to come by the boat:"

Notice these words, *'And when the ship was caught, and could not bear up into the wind, we let her drive.'* The moment you cut yourself off from the divine direction, you will get caught and lose control of your life's destiny. In their case they lost control of their ship. The interesting point I want to draw your attention to, is when Paul admonished them, *'Sirs, I perceive that this voyage will be with hurt and much damage, not only of the lading and ship, but also of our lives.'* How did Paul know this? He was a tent maker by trade and a preacher, he was not a weather man or a seasoned seaman. Yet he picked up on something that a professional could not pick up.

Paul's own words are very revealing, 'Sirs, I perceive...' To perceive means ' to discern, identify and detect'. In Greek it's the word, 'Theoreo' meaning 'to see or perceive with the eyes', 'to perceive with the inner man' but it also means 'God spoke'. We know this could not refer to physical eyes as the centurion and all those on the ship had eyes but could not see the situation ahead. In the natural, what Paul said was totally illogical to the captain of the boat. However Paul had tapped into God's mind. I want to remind you of what was written in the book of Job, 'For God speaketh once, yea twice, **yet man perceiveth it not.**

*'In a dream, in a vision of the night, when deep sleep falleth upon men, in slumberings upon the bed; Then he openeth the ears of men, and sealeth their instruction, That he may withdraw man from his purpose, and hide pride from man. He keepeth back his soul from the pit, and his life from perishing by the sword.'*(Job 33:14-19). Paul tapped into the voice of God to deliver him and those on board from death. It did not say that Paul heard the audible voice of God! He perceived it! He sensed it in his spirit. God communicated something in his spirit. He had a check in his spirit or a sense of uneasiness not to move forward. Here are two important tips,

*'Where there is no perception, deception will follow.'*

*'Where there is no perception, destruction will follow'*

Here are another two important tips,

*'Where there is perception, there will be protection.'*

*'Where there is perception, there will be preservation.'*

The captain of the ship overruled Paul's perception to his own hurt. He wrecked his boat and lost the goods on board that their very own hands had to throw overboard. This is to let you know when you are not led by the Spirit, you will lose your goods. It is vitally important for you to be like the apostle Paul, a man who was very accurate in the spirit. You also need to understand that Paul was not the only believer on the boat. There were at least two more who were with him, Aristarchus, who was a laborer and traveler with Paul, as well as the beloved physician, Dr Luke. Both of them did not pick up what Paul did.

As a matter of fact, Luke himself penned, 'And *when neither sun nor stars in many days appeared,* and no small tempest lay on us, *all hope that we should be saved was then taken away.'* (Acts 27:20) Luke thought this was the end of them. He had no hope! This brings an important point that two believers can be in the same situation and the same boat but they don't have the same frame of mind.

Luke was hopeless as he did not see the sun and stars but felt the battering of the storm, whereas Paul had already heard from God. One had death on his mind and the other had living on his mind. One could only pick up on the negativity of the natural while the other could pick up the direction of the Holy Spirit. How did Paul become that way? It is not because he was a super apostle. No, he trained himself to be that way. He fine-tuned his spirit man to hear the direction and voice of the Holy Spirit.

*Where there is no perception, deception will follow. Where there is no perception, destruction will follow*

It was only by the grace of God that Paul and the rest were saved. Paul was helpless to do anything about not going forward in that journey as he was not the one in charge of the boat. He happened to be traveling there because as a prisoner, he was dependent on the will of the centurion. The latter did not listen to Paul but the master of the ship. Paul was then subjected to a storm that he could have avoided. Sometimes we go through storms because of what others are doing. God will be gracious to help you when he knows that it is beyond your ability to heed his voice. The centurion overruled the voice of the Spirit and not Paul. That is why God sent his angel to deliver Paul. Now when it is within your capacity and power to listen and obey but you choose to disobey and overrule God's prompting, the result can be devastating. This is very important to grasp,

**When others overrule the voice of God on your behalf, you open yourself to the mercy of God.**

**When you overrule the voice of God, you open yourself to the malice of the devil.**

Paul is the one who taught us through his letters about the inward witness and how to be led by the Spirit. He taught us about the voice of conscience being the voice of your spirit guiding you.

**Romans 9:1; "I say the truth in Christ, I lie not, my conscience also bearing me witness in the Holy Ghost.."**

**Acts 24:16; "And herein do I exercise myself, to have always a conscience void of offence toward God, and toward men."**

Romans 2:14, 15; "For when the Gentiles, which have not the law, do by nature the things contained in the law, these, having not the law, are a law unto themselves:

Which shew the work of the law written in their hearts, *their conscience also bearing witness, and their thoughts the mean* while accusing or else excusing one another;'

Gleaning from the book of Acts and Paul's epistles, we see that this man was inclined to follow the inward witness of the Spirit. This is played out beautifully just before the Macedonian call,

Acts 16:6-Now when they had gone throughout Phrygia and the region of Galatia, and were *forbidden of the Holy Ghost* to preach the word in Asia, After they were come to Mysia, they assayed to go into Bithynia: *but the Spirit suffered them not.* And they passing by Mysia came down to Troas. And a vision appeared to Paul in the night; There stood a man of Macedonia, and prayed him, saying, Come over into Macedonia, and help us. And after he had seen the vision, immediately we endeavoured to go into Macedonia, assuredly gathering that the Lord had called us for to preach the gospel unto them. Therefore loosing from Troas, we came with a straight course to Samothracia, and the next day to Neapolis; And from thence to Philippi, which is the chief city of that part of Macedonia, and a colony: and we were in that city abiding certain days."

*'Forbidden of the Holy Ghost'*

*'The Spirit suffered them not'*

What is going on here? I thought Jesus said, 'Go ye into all the world and preach the Gospel to every creature...'(Mark 16:15) Is there a discrepancy between the Holy Spirit and Jesus? No, none at all. Jesus gave us the Great Commission of

Mark 16. Yes he did! But the Great Commission to go out into all the world, was given to the whole body of Christ and not to you single-handedly. You have to find out where God wants you to go. Paul made this remarkable statement, '..*the gospel of the uncircumcision was committed unto me, as the gospel of the circumcision was unto Peter.*' That seems to be the wrong way round. If it was me or you, we would have assigned Paul to the Jews and Peter to the Gentiles.

Logic would demand that, as that would be placing them in their field of strength. God chose the other way because he did not want them to rely on their own flesh and ability but to be led by the Spirit. When Paul wanted to go to Asia, the Holy Ghost forbade him. When he wanted to go to Bithynia, the Spirit did not allow him. How did that happen? The Holy Spirit was not standing there with a belt or stick threatening Paul. He knew it by the inward witness. He had a stop light in his spirit or a stop sign inside of him. Then it says, 'he assayed to go to Bithynia.' Assayed means that he tested, probed, examined assessed and analyzed and the answer came back to him as negative inside of him. He knew this was a 'no-no' for him.

The best way I can explain this is by reminding you of a game show that we see or have seen on television. In USA, it is called Family Feud and in England it is called Family Fortunes. I am sure you can remember. Two family teams, each with five members, would be asked to guess the results of surveys, in which 100 people would be asked open ended questions. The one who got the highest score will then play. Then they would have to find all the answers that were given in the survey.

Do you remember the sound that came when they got the wrong answer. If it was the right answer, there would be a 'ding' sound. Growing up in England, I used to love the sound of the wrong answer. It was double horrible buzz. Well sometimes you will have this 'double horrible buzz' sound in your belly and that means not to proceed. Needing to find out his next move God revealed it to him in a vision in the night. Once he found out where he was to go, he quickly moved on the instruction.

*When you overrule the voice of God, you open yourself to the malice of the devil*

The question you have to ask yourself is, 'How did Paul get that way?' Well the answer is very clear when he uttered these wonderful words, 'I thank my God that I speak in tongues more than ye all (1 Corinthians 14:18) That is why he commended the church to build themselves up by praying in the Holy Ghost.' The Apostle Paul fine-tuned his spirit man to the Spirit of God. He was a man who was conversant with the Word of God and with the Holy Spirit. In the next chapter I will show you how to train and fine-tune your spirit man like Paul. I will also give you some personal experiences from my own life to better help you.

RECEIVING DIRECTION FROM ABOVE

CHANGE 8

# FINE-TUNING THE HUMAN SPIRIT & PERSONAL EXPERIENCES

Your spirit needs to be trained just as your body needs to be trained to be in good shape. It is amazing how many people will diligently work out physically to be healthy and yet never work out spiritually so it may be well with them.

As a matter of fact, a person must have a program to develop spiritually, mentally and physically. Some people have never even heard of training the human spirit and yet it is very crucial to success in your Christian life. Without it, you become like this toy that you can see when you go to the shopping mall. I'm sure you have seen it. They have a little ferret operated by a battery with a little ball attached to its nose. It moves constantly without any sense of direction. It bumps into walls and keeps moving from one pillar to another post. It is forever moving and never getting anywhere, being pushed around by life's obstacles. It will keep on moving until its battery dies.

Some of you are old enough to remember when you were a child where we had toy cars or trains that will just go in one direction until they hit a wall. Then the wheels would keep spinning until it can get into a position free from the obstacle and head towards the next obstacle and the same thing happens over and over again. Unfortunately that is how many believers live today. Forever moving but never getting anywhere!

## *House hunting*

I remember in 2008, we wanted to buy and move into a bigger house in Louisville. When Rosanna and I decided to move into a bigger house, we were excited. So we contacted our realtor who is a friend of ours and we started looking at houses. We looked at so many houses and in so many different neighborhoods. We visited medium sized houses, big houses and very big houses. I was excited! Rosanna was excited! My kids were excited as we started on this new project. After about ten or more house visits and tours, my excitement was wearing off. The house I liked, my wife did not like. The houses she liked, I did not like. Then if the house was ideal, the neighborhood was not. If the neighborhood and house were ideal, the yard would be too big or too small.

After a while it became a burden to me to go visiting more houses. I can remember sitting on a plane going to London, England and thinking to myself, 'This is boring and tiring. I am done with this.' I remember the phone call I had with my wife while she was at home in USA and I was ministering in London. The realtor and her had more houses for me to visit with them when I arrived back home. I blurted out, 'I'm not going, I am done with visiting houses. It is too tiring and beside I don't like what you like and you don't like what I like.

I am bored with it.' Needless to say Rosanna was not impressed with me. My realtor talked to me while I was overseas, she is a personal friend and also a pastor. She asked me, 'Glenn, have you changed your mind? You don't want to move?' I explained to her, 'No, I have not changed my mind, it is just that I am not excited by it any more.' I am sure she was also not impressed with me but she did tell me to pray.

To tell you the truth, I put it on the shelf and forgot about it while I was in London. I could not be bothered to pray about house visits. It was only when I was on my way back to the USA, on the plane that I gave some thoughts to houses. Knowing that Rosanna would ask me about it once I'm home was my motivation to pray. I prayed out of exasperation, 'Lord, this is boring to me. I'm tired of visiting houses. I need a house that ticks all the boxes and for all of us to be happy about.' After praying about it, I just stayed quiet before the Lord. This question popped into my thinking.

'What neighborhood do you like?' I distinctly remember even before I moved my family to Louisville, my realtor was showing me some neighborhoods and as we drove by one particular neighborhood, I said, 'Lord, if I ever move to Louisville, this is the neighborhood I will stay.' I liked the peace, the houses and the scenery.

The reply came, 'Well then look for your house in that neighborhood.' When I arrived home, Rosanna asked me about some houses to go visit. I replied, 'No, we are not going to visit all these houses. I know where we are going to live.' This was during Thanksgiving time. I told her of the particular neighborhood and said, 'Let's go and see if there are any houses for sale there.' All the kids jumped in the car and off we went. On the way there, we called our realtor and told her that we wanted to buy a house in that neighborhood. She said she would look into it right away. As we entered the neighborhood, all of us were happy as we looked at the place and all the houses. Well, we drove through the whole neighborhood and there was no house for sale. The realtor called back and said there was no house for sale there. However this time I had a peace in my spirit. This was during Thanksgiving. As I drove away, I felt a small voice inside of me. The same small voice that spoke to me on the plane. I heard in my spirit, 'There will be a house for sale after Christmas' which I proceeded to tell Rosanna and the kids.

'How do you know?', they asked

'I know'

'Are we going to visit any more houses?'

'No, there will be one available after Christmas!'

As I mentioned this was during Thanksgiving in November. All through December I did not visit any houses. I did not even go back to that neighborhood, but the day after Christmas right after lunch, I told my wife and kids to jump in the car.

*Some people are forever moving but never getting anywhere. The voice of God will make a way for you*

'Where are we going?' They probably thought that we were going shopping. I said, 'We are going to see our new house.' Sure enough when we arrived, there was a house for sale as the Lord witnessed in my spirit. My wife fell in love with it. I loved it and my kids loved it. Today we are living in this house until we decide to move. But when we do, we won't go through the pain of visiting houses and more houses. We have learnt our lesson.

## *Audible voice of God*

When I was a teenager, I discovered the will of God for my life was to be a minister of the Gospel. After that I made a commitment to God that I would not run from girlfriend to girlfriend. I wanted to be with the person who he had for me. I prayed about it all the time. At that time of my life I was living in London, England. Our church had many young people and plenty of girls. Who do I go with? Is she the one or is this the one? It was quite a complex time. You know as teenagers even simple things are complex. I prayed and I prayed.

One day this man of God came to our church. His name was Michael McCann. It was a Tuesday night bible study in the summer. I was about seventeen years old . When he finished preaching, he was doing the altar call and moving in the gifts of the Spirit. All of a sudden he stopped and called me, 'Young man, come here.' I went forward, not knowing what was going to be said or done. He looked at me and said, 'Young man, the Lord says to you, Don't worry about your wife.' My first thought was,' he brought me out here to tell me this.' How embarrassing! He went on again, 'Young man, God says not to worry about your wife.'

Again my thought was, 'I'm not worried, if you just show me who she is, I'll be fine.' He continued, 'She, your wife, is not among you yet but soon you will know, it will be revealed to you.' I can tell you that I was not too impressed but I knew this man was a man of God. So I stopped thinking about it. One day as I was sleeping, I had a dream and in the dream I was getting married. I saw myself standing in the front of the church waiting for the bridal entry. Then I heard the music for the bride to enter and in my dream I looked back and saw this girl in a white dress walking towards me. She had a veil covering her face. In my dream I was saying to myself, 'Come on remove the veil, I want to see what you look like.' She came forward and stood by me and never removed the veil. As I was standing there in my dream, I heard the audible voice of God saying, 'Your wife's name will be Anna.' and then the dream finished. I woke up the next morning, on a mission to find Anna.

A few weeks later, school would start and when we were expecting new people to come to work in our church school. I was sitting on a chair minding my own business, being introduced to the new folks who came to work when this girl walked in. I had never seen her before. She was out of town. I thought to myself, 'Wow, she is pretty!' I never talked to her for some time. Then one day I asked her, 'What's your name?'

'Rosanna', she replied

I thought , 'Well Lord that's close enough'

*The Apostle Paul fine-tuned his spirit man to the Spirit of God. He was a man who was conversant with the Word of God and with the Holy Spirit*

It was only a little later when we started to date that I found out her real name on her birth certificate is Anna Rose. God does not make mistakes and we were married on the 17th March 1990.  Once I heard the voice of my God, there was no need for me to run helter-skelter looking for a woman to have me. The voice of God cuts the frustration out of your life.

## Kotoka International Airport

My very first ministry trip to mainland Africa was to the Cote D'Ivoire via Accra. I believe I was twenty- two years old. I was apprehensive and excited at the same time. I did not go with a group but by myself. I was to be in Abidjan for two weeks and after that on the way home, make a stopover in

Accra. After two weeks I was ready to come back home to be with my newly wedded wife. I was booked on Ghana Airways from Abidjan to Accra then change plane to go back home. As soon as we landed in Accra's Kotoka airport and deplaned, we were greeted by an immigration officer and border control agents who declared,

'Everybody who came from this plane is to be deported back to Abidjan. Not one of you will transfer to a connecting flight. You are all illegal immigrants!'

I protested, 'Sir, I am not Ivorian. I am not Ghanaian!'

The man looked at me and said, 'I have orders to put everyone back on that plane and send them back to Abidjan.'

I said, 'Sir, I am not Ivorian, I do not live in Abidjan, where will they put me when I land back in Abidjan.'

His reply, 'It's not my problem! If you are not Ivorian then they will put you in jail.'

As soon as he mentioned jail, my ears perked up. I have seen TV documentaries on African jail. This is not like American jail or European jail where people are well treated. My mind had pictures of beatings and torture. I tell you I began to pray in tongues like I had never prayer before. I did not care how loud it was and if I looked crazy. Here I am standing with other passengers in a detention place ready to be shipped to a country which is not my own. That immigration officer was bent on making sure I get on that plane. The more I reasoned with him, the angrier he became. He kept telling me, 'You! You will go back to Abidjan!'

I prayed in the spirit like I had never prayed before. If ever I needed the voice of God, it was that day. If ever I need direction from above it was that day. To make matters worst, while I was detained, my connecting flight departed. It looked and felt like a hopeless situation. But thank God for the Holy Ghost! As I prayed in tongues, I felt in my spirit to go to talk to an English man that I saw walking by. The more I prayed, the more I was prompted to go talk to this man. All the time my mind was telling me that it was futile but something inside of me kept nudging me to go.

As I went to talk to that gentleman, the immigration officer came running towards me screaming, 'You! Get back over there! I am sending you back to Abidjan.' Boldness came over me and I said, "I am not talking to you, I am talking to this man.' That officer kept shouting at me and I responded, 'I'm not talking to you.' The English guy heard the commotion and came towards me saying, 'Sir, how can I help you.' I explained to him the situation while the immigration officer yelled at both of us. The man asked me for my passport and I further explained that my connecting flight had already departed. When he took my passport and ticket, the officer began to yell at him. He came back fifteen minutes later with a brand new ticket on British Airways to send me back to London. The thing is, I never paid a ticket for British Airways. I was booked on Ghana Airways. God had this man to issue me a brand new ticket. As I sat on the plane that evening, I was so glad that I was baptized in the Holy Spirit and prayed in tongues. It led me to the right person to deliver me from the crazy immigration officer.

## Fine-Tuning Your spirit man

Here are some keys to train and fine-tune your spirit to the Holy Spirit.

**1- Make it your priority to know the Word.** Make the Word the first and final authority in your life. Remember the Word will give you the general guidance that you need.

Meditate upon the Logos so that it can become a Rhema to you when you need it. One day, you may step into a situation and all of a sudden a Scripture comes to your mind. What is this? That's a quickened Word that you need to defeat the circumstance. Solomon said, *'The spirit of man is the candle of the Lord, searching all the inward parts.'*(Proverbs 20:27)

What is your spirit looking for? It's looking for the Word that will deal with and overcome the circumstance. What if there is no Scripture there? Then you are in a world of hurt. It's like your computer. You have so many files and documents in it. Let's say you are looking for a particular document that you cannot find on your desktop. What do you do? You will go to your search engine. Press 'search' and wait while your computer looks for the particular file. Once it is done, it will say, 'Five files found 'with the title you are looking for. If it is not there, it will say 'Zero files found'. That is pretty much how your spirit operates. It is looking for something when you step into a situation. It is looking for a Scripture that can deal and overcome with the situation.

However, for so many believers, because they are saturated with the world and not the Word, what comes- up is zero promises found. You do not want to be in this position.

**2- Be a doer of the Word.** Be quick to act upon the Word of God. The quicker you are to act upon the Word, the quicker you will see the supernatural in your life. The miraculous is released the moment you act on the Word. Heaven will back you on the earth, the moment you decide to take God at his Word. Jesus said, 'The Scripture cannot be broken.'(John 10:35)

**3- Pray in tongues constantly.** It is a master key to being led by the Spirit. It will give your spirit man the ascendancy over your flesh. Praying in tongues will open you to the divine mysteries that God has for you. As you pray in the spirit, pay attention to the ideas, concepts and insights that well up from your spirit to your mind. Tongues will sensitize your spirit to the voice and direction of the Holy Spirit.

**4- Give yourself to regular fasting.** Some people have the idea, 'I will fast to get God to hear me.' In reality it is the other way around. A person fasts to hear from God. Fasting is a great way to stretch your spirit, soul and body. Jesus fasted as did Paul and other great men and women in the Scriptures. Use wisdom with an understanding of your physical makeup before you start fasting. If you have not fasted for one day, it is pointless for you to shoot for a forty day fast. Train yourself little by little. The quest of fasting is to shut down carnal voices and stretch your spirit to be sensitive to God.

**5- Follow the instruction that is impressed on your heart.**

Learn to follow and act upon the inner impression. If you start to recognize this inner promptings of the Spirit and act upon them, after a while you will become accustomed to his leading. The more that you do, the more confident and conversant you will be with the Holy Spirit. Learn to trust God in small things to be familiar with his voice in order for you to trust to hear his voice in big situations.

CHAPTER 9

# POSITIONING TO RECEIVE DIRECTION FROM ABOVE

As we come to this last chapter, I believe you are now ready and keen to tap into this glorious blessing of direction from above that belongs to every believer. It is His voice that makes the difference. Now that you understand the importance of heeding his direction and not to lean on the flesh, how do you posture yourself to hear this marvelous leading of the Spirit?

Many years ago, I realized that if I could hear the voice of the Holy Spirit in my inner man then I would be ahead of the devil and my enemies. As a teenager, I remember praying, 'Lord, talk to me!' That's all I repeated over and over again. Then this thought came to me, 'If you shut up and listen you might just hear him.' When I hushed down, it was far easier to hear him. So let me help you to properly position yourself to hear his bidding,

- **Humble yourself before him to receive instruction.**

You do not know it all! You are not less than a man when you don't know how to fix a certain situation. Many times our pride gets in the way and we want to fix it ourselves. It is

69

commendable that you want to fix the circumstance but there are some problems which are beyond your physical, educational, financial and intellectual capacity. Remember this powerful translation from the Message Bible, 'Trust God from the bottom of your heart; **don't try to figure out everything on your own.** Listen for God's voice in everything you do, everywhere you go; he's the one who will keep you on track. **Don't assume that you know it all. Run to God...**"(Proverbs 3:5-7) Meditate upon these words, '...*don't try to figure out everything on your own.*' Humble yourself before God! Tell him, 'Lord, I don't know how to fix this but you do. I come to you and humble myself before you to receive your instruction.' It does not matter if the problem arose because of your doing or someone else's bad move. You still go before God and ask him for instruction.

> Psalm 25:9, 14; "The meek will he guide in judgment: and the meek will he teach his way...The secret of the LORD is with them that fear him; and he will shew them his covenant.'

The fear of the Lord is the beginning of wisdom. Solomon told us that wisdom is the principal thing to acquire (Proverbs 4:7). What is wisdom? It is the voice of God. You cannot access his wisdom without the fear of the Lord. Now that does not mean that you are afraid of God but that you reverence him and humble yourself before his ways.

> Job 28:28; "And unto man he said, Behold, the fear of the Lord, that is wisdom; and to depart from evil is understanding.
>
> Psalm 34:11; "Come, ye children, hearken unto me: I will teach you the fear of the LORD."
>
> Psalm 111:10; "The fear of the LORD is the beginning of wisdom..."

Proverbs1:7; "The fear of the LORD is the beginning of knowledge: but fools despise wisdom and instruction.

Proverbs 8:13; "The fear of the LORD is to hate evil: pride, and arrogancy, and the evil way, and the froward mouth, do I hate".

**Proverbs 15:33; "The fear of the LORD is the instruction of wisdom; and before honor is humility."**

*You do not know it all! Humble Yourself and Run to God*

The fear of the Lord and humility go together. The moment you humble yourself, you have positioned yourself correctly to hear his instruction. This simply means, 'Not my way Lord, but your way.'

- **Walk away from sin.**

Sin separates you from God. Let me mark your thinking with these words.

*Sin will separate you from the person of God.*

*Fear will separate you from the power of God.*

*Doubt and unbelief will separate you from the promises of God.*

If you are walking in sin, it will dull your ears to hear from God. Be quick to repent. You see repentance will position you correctly before God.

- **Create an atmosphere of praise around and in you.**

It is important for you to understand that God inhabits the praises of his people. That means God's presence is attracted when we have an attitude of praise. Moaning and griping will not get the attention of God. No one wants to spend time with a sourpuss and neither does God. When you read the Bible, especially the Old Testament, you will discover God did not like people who murmured and moaned. The Psalmist brings this point clearly, 'And they sinned yet more against him by *provoking the most High in the wilderness.* And they tempted God in their heart by asking meat for their lust. *Yea, they spake against God;* they said, Can God furnish a table in the wilderness? Behold, he smote the rock, that the waters gushed out, and the streams overflowed; can he give bread also? can he provide flesh for his people? *Therefore the Lord heard this, and was wroth:* so a fire was kindled against Jacob, and anger also came up against Israel.'(Psalm 78:17-21) God himself had something to say about murmuring,

Numbers 14:27; "How long shall I bear with this evil congregation, which murmur against me? I have heard the murmurings of the children of Israel, which they murmur against me."

You will not attract God if all you do is complain, gripe and moan. You certainly will not be in a position to hear his voice. If you want to hear his voice then you need to be in a place of praise and thanksgiving. Isaiah substantiates this thought,

Isaiah 30:29, 30; "*Ye shall have a song,* as in the night when a holy solemnity is kept; *and gladness of heart,* as when one goeth with a pipe to come into the mountain of the Lord, to the mighty One of Israel. *And the Lord shall cause his glorious voice to be heard,* and shall shew the lighting down of his arm, with the indignation of his anger, and with the flame of a devouring fire, with scattering, and tempest, and hailstones."

**You shall have a song**

**Gladness of heart**

**The Lord shall cause his glorious voice to be heard**

The voice of the Lord will be heard when you have a song in your heart and gladness of heart. You cannot hear God when you are bitter and resentful. So have a praise in your heart and in your mouth. Attract God with your attitude of praise. Put a praise and worship c.d. in your car and house at all times. There is something about praise that will open you up to hear the voice of the Lord. There is a powerful story in the Old Testament that shows us the value of praise to hear the instruction of the Lord. When evil King Jehoram of Israel was facing an imminent attack from the King of Moab, he summoned good King Jehoshaphat of Judah to come to his help. Jehoram did not see a way out his predicament and he was in despair, but Jehoshaphat knew what to do,

> **2 Kings 3:10-16; "And the king of Israel said, Alas! that the LORD hath called these three kings together, to deliver them into the hand of Moab!** *But Jehoshaphat said, Is there not here a prophet of the LORD, that we may enquire of the LORD by him?* **And one of the king of Israel's servants answered and said, Here is Elisha the son of Shaphat, which poured water on the hands of Elijah.** *And Jehoshaphat said, The word of the LORD is with him.* **So the king of Israel and Jehoshaphat and the king of Edom went down to him. And Elisha said unto the king of Israel, What have I to do with thee? get thee to the prophets of thy father, and to the prophets of thy mother. And the king of Israel said unto him, Nay: for the LORD hath called these three kings together, to deliver them into the hand of Moab. And Elisha said, As the LORD of hosts liveth, before whom I stand, surely, were it not that I regard the presence of Jehoshaphat the king of Judah, I would not look toward thee, nor see thee.** *But now bring me a minstrel. And it came to pass, when the minstrel played, that the hand of the LORD came upon him. And he said, Thus saith the LORD,* **Make this valley full of ditches..."**

Jehoshaphat needed direction from the Lord to win the

*You cannot hear God when you are bitter and resentful.*

battle. Elisha, the prophet of God was summoned to bring the Word of the Lord. However Elisha needed that the Holy Spirit should come upon him to inspire him with prophetic utterances.

Remember the New Testament said, "For the prophecy came not in old time by the will of man: but holy men of God spake as they were moved by the Holy Ghost.'(2 Peter 1:21) Elisha needed the Holy Ghost to move upon him and what did he do. He said, 'Bring me a minstrel..." When the minstrel played, Elisha then picked up on the voice of the Lord. This is a very important point! Music anointed of the Holy Ghost opens you up to the voice of God. It will open your spiritual ears to the Lord to instruct you how to win the battle. That's the reason you must always have an attitude of praise. Protect your atmosphere.

Don't let doubt and fear dominate your environment. You create your atmosphere in which you want to live. In an atmosphere of doubt and fear you open yourself up to the voice of the devil but in an atmosphere of praise and thanksgiving, you will hear God. The choice is yours!

Life becomes a great adventure when you receive direction

*Music anointed of the Holy Ghost opens you up to the voice of God. It will open your spiritual ears to the Lord to instruct you how to win the battle.*

from above. Let your life soar to new heights as you allow yourself to be led by the Spirit. Jesus said, 'My sheep knows my voice.' You are his sheep and it is your God given right to know this amazing voice.

**Isaiah 30:21 says, "And thine ears shall hear a word behind thee, saying, This**

is the way, walk ye in it, when ye turn to the right hand,
and when ye turn to the left.

Then listen to the promptings of your spirit from the Holy
Spirit. As long as you do not hear from heaven, don't move. As
soon as you hear directions from above, MOVE! You will see
the supernatural.

# WE WANT TO
# HEAR FROM YOU

***Contact Details***

Glenn Arekion Ministries

PO Box 197777

Louisville, KY 40259

USA

www.glennarekion.org

# People Like You...
## Make People Like Me... Go!

*Also I heard the voice of the Lord, saying, Whom shall I send, and who will go for us? Then said I, Here am I; send me. And he said, Go, and tell this people*

ISAIAH 6:8

Now more than ever there is a need for laborers in the kingdom of God. I have faithfully been serving the Master on the mission field for more than 25 years. It is an honor for me to be on active duty for the Lord Jesus Christ. I wear his emblem and reproach gladly. The vision which the Lord gave me was to preach the uncompromising Word of God to the nations with an emphasis on the supernatural. This is why Glenn Arekion Ministries spends hundreds of thousands of dollars roaming the nations in crusades, conventions and seminars.

## I NEED YOU TO PARTNER WITH ME

Partnership in ministry is not a new concept, nor is it a scam for preachers to get money from you. You may ask, 'What is a partner and why do you need partners?'

❖ A partner is a person who partakes of the vision of another, enabling him to fulfill what he believes God has called him to do.
❖ A partner is one who sows financially and prayerfully into a ministry to help fulfill their mandate from God.
❖ A partner is one who provides provision for the vision.
❖ A partner is one who ministers of his/her financial substance helping the ministry to go through cities and nations to minister of their spiritual substance.

## Examples of partnership in ministry

As just mentioned partnership is not a new concept. Even Jesus and Paul had partners in ministry aiding them to complete his Father's business.

## Jesus

*And it came to pass afterward, that he went throughout every city and village, preaching and shewing the glad tidings of the kingdom of God: and the twelve were with him, And certain women, which had been healed of evil spirits and infirmities, Mary called Magdalene, out of whom went seven devils, And Joanna the wife of Chuza Herod's steward, and Susanna, and many others, which ministered unto him of their substance.*

LUKE 8:1-3

It may be that you cannot go to the mission field physically but you can still be involved in the Great Commission by partnering financially and prayerfully with Glenn Arekion Ministries as we travel the earth preaching the glad tidings of the kingdom. In fact every believer must partner with a ministry or the local church for the spreading of the good news of Jesus Christ. This is even more true today as we can see how desperately wicked and evil our world is becoming.

## Paul

*Now ye Philippians know also, that in the beginning of the gospel, when I departed from Macedonia, no church communicated with me as concerning giving and receiving, but ye only. For even in Thessalonica ye sent once and again unto my necessity. Not because I desire a gift: but I desire fruit that may abound to your account.*

PHILIPPIANS 4:15-17

# GOSPEL PARTNERS

For Paul to fulfill his missionary journeys he needed the financial partnership of the Philippian church. As you can see a partner can either be an individual or a church financially partnering with a ministry to fulfill its mission obligations. We also see that Paul says, 'I desire fruit to abound to your account' meaning when we are actively involved in the spreading of the Gospel, our heavenly bank account is increasing both in terms of souls and monies.

**Glenn Arekion Ministries** has a mandate to reach the masses through:

❖ Television outreaches – National and international TV outreaches (The Word Network, Faith TV USA and Faith TV Africa).
❖ Miracle crusades.
❖ Believer's conventions.
❖ Literature.
❖ Social media.

Apart from our television outreaches, Glenn Arekion literally travels thousands of miles yearly to Africa, Europe, North and South America as well as the islands, holding:

❖ Salvation and healing crusades.
❖ Holy Spirit seminars.
❖ Healing schools.
❖ Conventions.

He does so at *no cost* to the host nations or churches. In other words, Glenn Arekion does not demand a set fee to minister in any church, crusade or convention. He does not ask for travel costs either. Everything that Glenn Arekion Ministries does is solely at the cost of Glenn Arekion Ministries itself. This is why we need you as financial partners.

# GOSPEL PARTNERS

Not all of us have a call to go to the nations and preach the Gospel but ALL OF US have the responsibility to finance the spreading of the Gospel to save as many as we can, lest hell claims a multitude. Like Amos, you may feel,

> *...I was no prophet, nor was I a son of a prophet, but I was a sheep breeder and a tender of sycamore fruit. The the Lord took me as i followed the flock, and the Lord said to me, 'Go...'*
> Amos 7:14, 15

You may not be a prophet or an evangelist but you go when you send the evangelist or the prophet. My plea to you today is, 'Send me, I am ready to go...'

Our desire to reach the masses has not diminished BUT neither have the costs of declaring the Gospel via the different means. Today I am asking you to become covenant member of this ministry –a Gospel Partner. No financial gift is too big or too small. Every soul saved will equally also be your reward. Every healing that takes place will equally also be your reward.

## Become a Partner with Glenn Arekion Ministries

Visit **glennarekion.org/partner** today and join us!

# *Watch Dr Glenn on television every week*

Dr Glenn Arekion can be seen on television each week through the Faithlift TV Show, aired on The Word Network, Faith TV USA and Faith TV Africa.

You can also watch Faithlift on:

*Vimeo*: http://vimeo.com/glennarekion

*YouTube*: http://youtube.com/c/FaithliftTV

*Dr Glenn's website*: http://glennarekion.org/faithlift

# Further books by Dr Glenn Arekion...

## Available online at glennarekion.org
*Download eBooks and MP3 messages instantly*

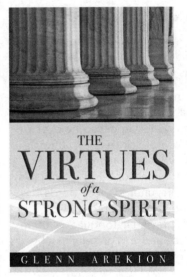

God created man with words of dominion and His original intent was for man to live from the inside out. This simply means to dominate the flesh from the spirit, and the natural from the spiritual. Since the fall of Adam, man has been living from his flesh, dominated by circumstances. Through the regeneration, our spirit man was reborn to win but the key is to know how to have a strong spirit. The stronger we are in our spirit the easier it will be for us to resist the attacks of the devil.

Living in the last days, it is imperative for the believer to be strong in spirit, to overcome the relentless attacks of the world, the flesh and the devil. Paul, the apostle, commanded the Ephesian believers to be 'Strong in the Lord'. How does one do that? He is not talking about our physical muscles. It is in the working out of our spirit man that we can truly be strong.

This book will unveil the secrets of spiritual strength and the consequences of having a weak spirit, such as:

- The stronger you are in your spirit, the more miracles and breakthroughs you will experience.
- The stronger you are in your spirit, the easier it will be for you to resist the attacks of the devil.
- The stronger you are in your spirit, the healthier you will be in your body.
- The stronger you are in your spirit, the less influence the world will have over you.

# Further books by Dr Glenn Arekion...

## Available online at glennarekion.org
*Download eBooks and MP3 messages instantly*

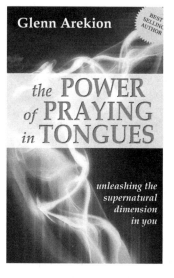

**Are you ready for the supernatural?**

Tired of mundane, dead Christianity and want to see Bible days in your life? Then this book is for you!

"I thank my God, I speak with tongues more than ye all" (1 Corinthians 14:18). Paul, the greatest apostle who ever lived, who wrote close to two-thirds of the New Testament and gave you your foundations for living an effective Christian life, uttered these words. This founding father of the faith deemed "praying in tongues" of utmost importance and was grateful that he partook of such a great blessing.

Prayer is a command and calling of God. The Lord Jesus Christ specifically mentioned that His house is to be the house of prayer.

If you are born again, then you form part of the family of God, and prayer is your calling.

In The Power of Praying in Tongues, you will learn:

- The importance of praying in tongues
- Sixty expository benefits of praying in tongues
- The roots of negativism concerning tongues
- To develop partnership with the Holy Spirit
- To tap into supernatural Christianity

# Further books by Dr Glenn Arekion...

## Available online at glennarekion.org
*Download eBooks and MP3 messages instantly*

**Does the sight of blood scare you? Make you shudder? Cause you to feel faint?**

A childhood experience left Dr Glenn feeling this way for years – until he focused on the "precious blood of Christ" that provides eternal life and love.

Throughout time, the world has searched for the keys of protection and redemption. Every type of ritual, performance, and self-abasement imaginable has been attempted in this search while the true key has been overlooked.

The much neglected and noticeably overlooked subject of the blood of Christ trickling down the cross, which held captive His out-of-joint but unbroken body, is the answer that all of mankind has been waiting for. There are inexhaustible benefits of this uncommon blood; but before we can ever experience these benefits, we must first not only acknowledge them but also explore their possibilities.

This blood holds within it manifold blessings because of the covenant which it represents, whether it is approached for the salvation of a loved one, forgiveness of sin, or when the storms of life come upon us. This book will show you a step-by-step process to the victory in life that the precious blood of Christ holds. May Heaven kiss you and grant you its favor as you dig deeply into these anointed words.

# Further books by Dr Glenn Arekion...

## Available online at glennarekion.org
*Download eBooks and MP3 messages instantly*

What you are about to read will revolutionize your life and take you to a higher dimension! The anointing is the most indispensable force in the life of the believer. With it, you will have the power and faith to do great exploits. Without it, life and ministry will be a constant source of frustration and irritation. Many have visions but simply do not know how to make the realities in their lives.

This book is full of answers to your most frustrating questions. The name of the game is results, and when you know how to purposely tap into the anointing and treasure of God, you will:

- Be transformed into a different person
- Be elevated into a new place in God
- Be the catalyst for positive change in the lives of suffering people
- See your dream become your destiny

Seven ways to increase your anointing will answer your heart's cry. It will show you how to remove the powerlessness and lack of influence in your life, while empowering you to do the mighty works of God.

# Further books by Dr Glenn Arekion...

## Available online at glennarekion.org
*Download eBooks and MP3 messages instantly*

Jesus declared that healing is the children's bread. It is the divine right of every believer to walk in divine healing, divine health and divine life. However, as long as there are questions in your mind as to whether or not it is God's will to heal, your faith will be hampered from receiving what Jesus legally purchased for you.

Since Jesus Christ is the same yesterday, today and forever, He is still anointed to heal. The ministry of Jesus, today, is still a miraculous, healing ministry - as it was when he first walked the streets of Jerusalem and the shores of Galilee.

This book will answer the important healing questions and reveal God's thoughts towards your wellness. This book will eliminate doubts, banish fear and boost your faith to receive your inheritance. As you meditate upon the truths in these chapters, you will discover:

- Did healing pass away with the apostles?
- Is God glorified through sickness?
- Am I entitled to divine health in old age?
- How to resist sickness
- How to receive your healing
- 101 healing promises
- Daily healing confessions to cover your life

His Word is medicine to our flesh. He sent His Word and His Word healed them all. You are part of the "all" He sent his Word to heal. Receive your healing NOW!

# Further books by Dr Glenn Arekion...

## Available online at glennarekion.org

*Download eBooks and MP3 messages instantly*

The apostle Paul had an understanding of the new creation like no other authors of the New Testament. What was passed on in the first Adam is now passed away in the last Adam! A revelation of the new creation in Christ will revolutionize your life. New-creation realities will enable you to dominate the old creation, that is the old man. In this powerful book, Dr Glenn Arekion unveils the power of the new man over the old man and the mindset of Paul by the explanation of:

- The finished work of Christ
- The curse of the law
- The blessing of Abraham
- The believer's position
- The realities of the new creation

Break free from the fallen genetics of the first Adam passed down to the human race and live from your new identity in Christ. This book will enlighten your understanding to your position in Jesus Christ. No longer will you accept the lies of the devil as the norms in your life.

Enjoy your new status in Christ over all the works of the enemy and walk in victory.

# Further books by Dr Glenn Arekion...

## Available online at glennarekion.org
*Download eBooks and MP3 messages instantly*

'I'm living the dream' is an expression that is often said but hardly ever experienced. Much has been said in the past years about the importance of dreams and visions for a fulfilled life and yet there are more dissatisfied people today than ever. This is because without wisdom, strategies and disciplines, visions remain grounded. Many have not reached the lofty positions that their dreams had for them due to a lack of these three fundamental forces.

Solomon, the most successful entrepreneurial king, knew the keys to success and he said in Ecclesiastes, 'For a dream cometh through the multitude of business...' Modern translations render this verse as, 'A dream comes through by much business, much activities and painful efforts.' Sitting down and merely having a dream without activities, strategies and certain disciplines implemented in your life will not trigger your dream to materialize.

This book explains the necessary wisdom strategies and the corresponding disciplines that you need to turn your dreams into realities. In this book you will learn:

- You are the number one enterprise that you need to build
- To destroy the excuses people use to abort their destiny
- The values of goals and diversities of goals
- Time management
- The ten characteristics of the diligent
- The million dollar habits you need to develop
- Wisdom secrets from the ants, the conies, the locusts and the spiders
- To turn your dreams into realities

# Further books by Dr Glenn Arekion...

## Available online at glennarekion.org
*Download eBooks and MP3 messages instantly*

You are only as effective as the quality of the information you receive. As a believer, you will be empowered, enlightened and energized as the exciting truths become alive in your heart and mind.

This book is a toolbox for the believer and minister, equipping them to fix life's problems. Life and ministry without the Holy Spirit, the Supernatural and His gifts will be a cycle of frustration but with Him actively involved, Bible results will become your reality!

If you are tired of living your Christian life without results then you need this great tool in your hands TODAY.

Through this book, Dr Glenn helps you:

- To develop your relationship with the greatest partner – The Holy Spirit
- To attract an active partnership with the Holy Spirit
- To grasp the purpose and validity of the gifts of the Spirit
- How to activate the gifts in your life and ministry
- To know what Paul meant by 'the best gift'
- To understand what the supernatural means
- To release the supernatural in your life and ministry
- To delve into 101 benefits of praying Tongues
- To understand the efficacy of fasting for a supernatural ministry
- To keep the fire of God burning in your life

This book contains 13 powerful chapters that will help you in your walk with God.

# Further books by Dr Glenn Arekion...

## Available online at glennarekion.org
*Download eBooks and MP3 messages instantly*

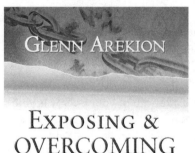

The first prophetic words ever spoken to humanity by Elohim were, "Be fruitful and multiply". Barrenness therefore is a direct assault, confrontation, violation and challenge to God's first decree to mankind. In this book you will discover that barrenness is not only a biological or a female problem and it operates on many different levels with different facets.

Barrenness is manifested:

- Biologically
- Territorially
- Financially
- Ministerially
- Generationally
- Mentally
- Professionally
- Spiritually
- Personally

When dealing with the spirit of barrenness, you are dealing with the spirit of stagnation and limitation. It seeks to curtail your life, your status, your ministry, your church, your family and your finances.

BUT IT CAN BE BROKEN!

In this book, Dr. Glenn gives you five powerful keys to destroy the spirit of barrenness and forbid it from ever operating in your life.

# Further books by Dr Glenn Arekion...

## Available online at glennarekion.org
*Download eBooks and MP3 messages instantly*

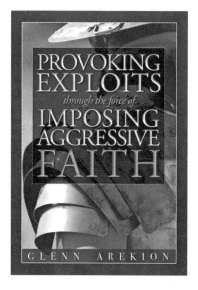

*And such as do wickedly against the covenant shall he corrupt by flatteries: but the people that do know their God shall be strong, and do exploits - Daniel 11:32*

**The strength of your enemy is your ignorance.** Those who are weak and ignorant will be exploited but those who are strong will have exploits. An exploit is a great feat that brings joy and every believer is called to a life of unlimited exploits - yet not every believer is experiencing this quality of life. Why? There are some key life-elements and attributes that are likely missing. Using Daniel 11:32 as the foundational verse, you will learn the prophecy and the history that this verse refers to. From the text, Glenn unravels five key attributes the believer must have in order to lead a life of exploits, specifically:

- Knowing God
- Being strong
- Having Imposing, aggressive faith
- Persistent and importunate prayer
- The leading of the Spirit

For many believers, the time span between exploits is too long. The Scripture says, *'Blessed be the Lord, who daily loadeth us with benefits...'* (Psalm 68:19).

Therefore we can have daily exploits. Many books have been written about faith but this book will open up another vista that will boost your faith for supernatural exploits. These five attributes - when implemented in your life - will set you up for exploits. No longer will you be exploited!

# Your notes...

# Your notes...

........................................................................................

........................................................................................

........................................................................................

........................................................................................

........................................................................................

........................................................................................

........................................................................................

........................................................................................

........................................................................................

........................................................................................

........................................................................................

........................................................................................

# Your notes...

# Your notes...

..............................................................................................

..............................................................................................

..............................................................................................

..............................................................................................

..............................................................................................

..............................................................................................

..............................................................................................

..............................................................................................

..............................................................................................

..............................................................................................